GETTING TO KNOW THE WORLD'S GREATEST ARTISTS

R O Y
LICHTENSTEIN

WRITTEN AND ILLUSTRATED BY MIKE VENEZIA

CHILDREN'S PRESS®
A DIVISION OF SCHOLASTIC INC.
NEW YORK TORONTO LONDON AUCKLAND SYDNEY
MEXICO CITY NEW DELHI HONG KONG
DANBURY, CONNECTICUT

Bobby, this book's for you!
Thanks for your wise words and the joy you've brought into our lives.
Love, Mike

Cover: *Blam*!, by Roy Lichtenstein. 1962. Oil on canvas. 68 x 80 in. © Estate of Roy Lichtenstein.

Colorist for illustrations: Kathy Pelot

Library of Congress Cataloging-in-Publication Data

Venezia, Mike.
    Roy Lichtenstein / written and illustrated by Mike Venezia.
      p. cm. — (Getting to know the world's greatest artists)
    ISBN 0-516-22030-6 (lib. bdg.)   0-516-25963-6 (pbk.)
    1. Lichtenstein, Roy, 1923.—Juvenile literature. 2. Artists—United States—
Biography—Juvenile literature. 3. Pop art—United States—Juvenile literature.
    [1. Lichtenstein, Roy, 1923- 2. Artists. 3. Pop art. 4. Art appreciation.]
    I. Lichtenstein, Roy, 1923- . ill. II. Title.
    N6537.L5V462001
    709'.2—dc21
                                    00-057030

Copyright 2001 by Mike Venezia.
All rights reserved. Published simultaneously in Canada.
Printed in the United States of America.
1 2 3 4 5 6 7 8 9 10 R 10 09 08 07 06 05 04 03 02 01

Roy Lichtenstein was born in New York City in 1923. Along with artists Andy Warhol, James Rosenquist, Claes Oldenburg, and a few others, he helped create Pop Art. This was one of the brightest and most fun periods of art ever!

Roy Lichtenstein's most famous paintings
are pictures of ideas he got from bubble-gum
wrappers, comic books, newspaper ads, and
even the yellow pages of the phone book!

Girl With Ball,
by Roy Lichtenstein.
1961. Oil on canvas.
60 1/2 x 36 1/2 in.
© Estate of Roy
Lichtenstein.

Sponge II, by Roy Lichtenstein. 1962. Oil on canvas. 36 x 36 in. © Estate of Roy Lichtenstein.

Using his special sense of humor and artistic skill, Roy Lichtenstein took popular images that people saw every day and made them into works of art. The name Pop Art came from the word "popular."

Step-on Can With Leg, by Roy Lichtenstein. 1961. Oil on canvas. 2 panels, 32 1/2 x 26 1/2 in. each.
© Estate of Roy Lichtenstein.

Baked Potato, by Roy Lichtenstein. 1962. Oil on canvas. 24 x 36 in. © Estate of Roy Lichtenstein.

Roy Lichtenstein had always been interested in drawing, science, and the way mechanical things worked. While growing up, he read all kinds of science magazines. Television hadn't been invented yet, so kids listened to radio programs instead. Roy loved listening to the science-fiction radio adventures of Flash Gordon.

Luckily, Roy lived near his favorite museum, the American Museum of Natural History. It was filled with information about dinosaurs, stars, planets, mummies, bugs, animals, and plants. Roy spent hours exploring the exhibits and great hallways of the museum.

Washington Crossing the Delaware, by Emanuel Gottlieb Leutze. 1851. Oil on canvas. 149 x 255 in.
© Metropolitan Museum of Art, Gift of John Stewart Kennedy, 1897.

During high school, Roy became more interested in art than ever. Since his school didn't offer any art classes, he decided to take lessons on his own.

It was during this time that Roy made up his mind to be an artist. Roy studied art in college, and after graduating, he became an art teacher. This allowed him to earn a living while he painted and showed his work.

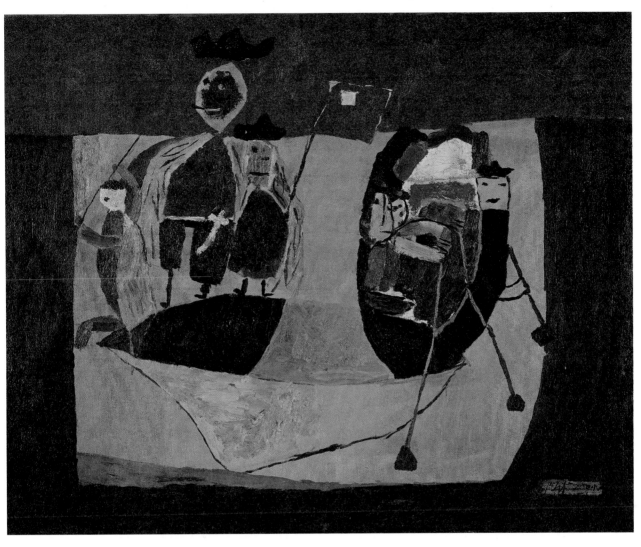

Washington Crossing the Delaware I, by Roy Lichtenstein. 1951. Oil on canvas. 26 x 32 in.
© Estate of Roy Lichtenstein.

Some of the first paintings he exhibited were
abstract versions of American historical
events and legends.

The Red Armchair, by Pablo Picasso. Spanish, 1881-1973. 1931. Oil on panel. 130.8 x 99 cm. © Art Institute of Chicago, Gift of Mr. and Mrs. Saidenberg/ Estate of Pablo Picasso/Artists Rights Society (ARS), New York.

Roy's early paintings were influenced by such great artists as Pablo Picasso and Fernand Léger. Roy liked the way these artists used thick outlines, flat shapes, and solid colors.

The Trapezists, by Fernand Léger. 1953. © Art Resource, NY, Private Collection/Artists Rights Society (ARS), New York/ADAGP, Paris.

In a way, many of these artists' paintings had the same qualities as comic-book art.

Roy was also interested in the most familiar art style of the 1950s, Abstract Expressionism.

Easter Monday, by Willem de Kooning. 1955-56. Oil and newspaper transfer on canvas. 96 x 74 in. © Metropolitan Museum of Art, Rogers Fund, 1956/Willem de Kooning Revocable Trust/Artists Rights Society (ARS), New York.

Abstract Expressionists like Jackson Pollock and Willem de Kooning used wild brush strokes, often splattering and dripping paint across their canvases. They did this to show their innermost feelings.

It took a long time for people to get used to Abstract Expressionist art. Once they did, though, it seemed like it was the only style of painting anyone cared about.

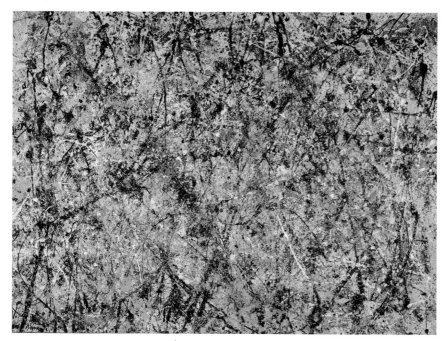

Number 1, 1950 (Lavender Mist), by Jackson Pollock. 1950. Oil, enamel and aluminum on canvas. 87 x 118 in. © National Gallery of Art, Washington, DC, Ailsa Mellon Bruce Fund, Richard Carafelli/Pollock-Krasner Foundation/Artists Rights Society (ARS), New York.

Artists everywhere were painting in this easy-to-copy style. Even though Roy Lichtenstein was interested in Abstract Expressionism, he felt it was being used way too much.

Look Mickey, by Roy Lichtenstein. 1961. Oil on canvas. 48 x 69 in. © Estate of Roy Lichtenstein.

Roy started looking for new and different ways to paint. He liked to look at bubble-gum wrappers and comic books with his sons. One day, just for fun, he made a large painting of a funny cartoon with Mickey Mouse and Donald Duck in it.

Roy was careful to make sure his colors looked flat and smooth, without any brush marks. He wanted this painting to look like it was mechanically printed, so it would be exactly the opposite of an Abstract Expressionist painting.

Roy even added little printer dots, called Benday dots, to give his painting more of a printed, cartoonlike look. When it was finished, Roy was surprised to find that he had made a painting that was exciting and different!

Popeye, by Roy Lichtenstein. 1961. Oil on canvas.
42 x 56 in. © Estate of Roy Lichtenstein.

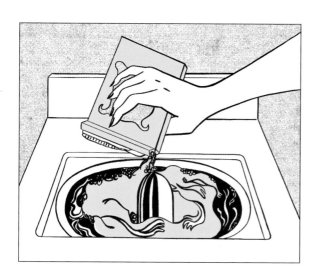

Washing Machine, by Roy Lichtenstein.
1961. Oil on canvas. 56 x 68 in.
© Estate of Roy Lichtenstein.

Roy Lichtenstein went to work making more paintings of ideas he got from comic books and newspaper ads. He took his paintings to a well-known art dealer in New York.

Leo Castelli appreciated new ideas in art.
He loved the fresh, exciting paintings Roy
showed him. Amazingly, at almost the exact
same time, a young artist named Andy Warhol
also brought Leo some comic-book paintings.
Leo Castelli suddenly realized that something
very important was beginning to happen in
the world of art.

Campbell's Soup I (Beef), by Andy Warhol. 1968. Screenprint on white paper. 35 x 23 in. © Art Resource, NY/ The Andy Warhol Foundation for the Arts/ARS, New York.

In 1962, Leo Castelli decided to put on a show of Roy Lichtenstein's paintings. It was one of the first Pop Art exhibits ever. Except for a few artist friends of Roy's, most people hated the show!

Other Pop artists were beginning to show their work at this time, too.

Andy Warhol decided to paint soup cans instead of comic-book pictures, and Claes Oldenburg was making giant fast-food sculptures. Some art critics felt they were looking at things in Pop-Art exhibits that they were forced to look at in the supermarket. They thought Pop Art wasn't serious at all, and a big waste of time!

Floor Burger, by Claes Oldenburg. 1962. painted sailcloth stuffed with foam. 132.1 x 213.4 cm. © Art Gallery of Ontario, Toronto. Reprinted with permission of Claes Oldenburg.

The Engagement Ring, by Roy Lichtenstein. 1961. Oil on canvas. 67 3/4 x 79 1/2 in.
© Estate of Roy Lichtenstein.

"Engagement Ring" panel from the comic strip "Winnie Winkle," by Martin Branner. 1961.
© Tribune Media Services, Inc. Reprinted with Permission.

At first, most people thought Roy Lichtenstein just took the comic-book images he found and blew them up to surprising sizes. If you look closely at the pictures he took his ideas from, though, you can see that Roy changed just about everything. The careful changes he made to the composition, color, thickness of lines, talk balloons, and Benday dots are what make his paintings important works of art.

Benday dots became Roy Lichtenstein's
trademark. This dot process was invented
by printer Benjamin Day in 1879. In comic
books and newspaper comic strips, it is used
as an inexpensive way of printing shades
and color tints.

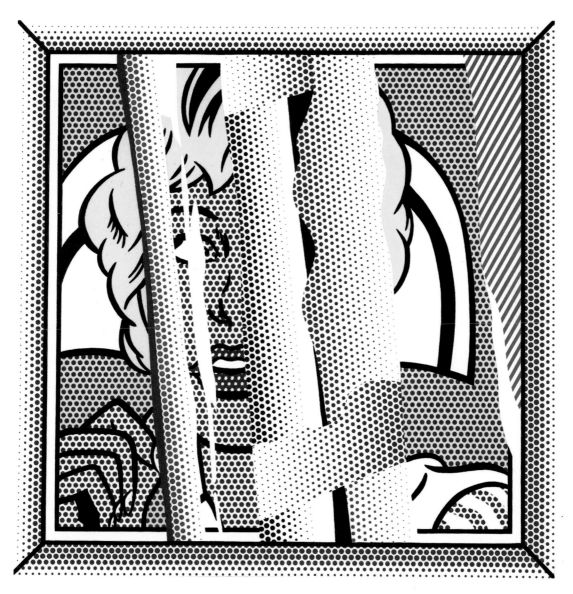

Reflections: Nurse, by Roy Lichtenstein. 1988. Oil and magna on canvas. 57 1/4 x 57 1/4 in.
© Estate of Roy Lichtenstein.

No one had ever made paintings using Benday dots before. In comic books, these dots aren't meant to be noticed, but Roy liked the way they looked and made them an important part of his paintings.

I Can See the Whole Room and There's Nobody in it . . ., by Roy Lichtenstein. 1961. Oil and graphite on canvas. 48 x 48 in. © Estate of Roy Lichtenstein.

It didn't take long for people to start appreciating Roy's art. Serious art critics soon realized that Pop paintings and sculptures were as important as any other style of art.

Girl With Hair Ribbon, by Roy Lichtenstein. 1965. Oil and magna on canvas. 48 x 48 in. © Estate of Roy Lichtenstein.

Lots of people thought Roy's paintings were just plain fun to look at, and easier to understand than Abstract Expressionist art.

Women Singing II, by Willem De Kooning. 1966. Oil on paper. 914 x 610 mm. © Art Resource, NY, Tate Gallery, London/ Willem de Kooning Revocable Trust/Artists Rights Society (ARS), New York.

27

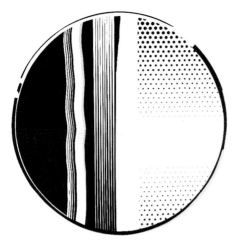

Mirror #3 (24" diameter), by Roy Lichtenstein.
1970. Oil and magna on canvas. 24 in. diameter.
© Estate of Roy Lichtenstein.

Interior With Mirrored Wall, by Roy Lichtenstein. 1991. Oil and
magna on canvas. 126 x 160 in. © Estate of Roy Lichtenstein.

As time went on, Roy Lichtenstein began painting different subjects. He made pictures of mirrors, room interiors, and decorations on buildings. He even made paintings of brush strokes! Although he moved away from his comic-book art, Roy almost always kept strong black lines, flat bright colors, and Benday dots as part of his paintings.

Entablature, by Roy Lichtenstein. 1974.
Magna, aluminum powder, beach
sand and magna medium on canvas.
60 x 100 in. © Estate of Roy
Lichtenstein.

Brushstrokes, by Roy Lichtenstein. 1965. Oil and magna on canvas. 48 x 48 in.
© Estate of Roy Lichtenstein.

Roy Lichtenstein also made other types of artwork. Some of his fun sculptures look like 3-D comic-book images that have jumped off the page.

I Love Liberty, by Roy Lichtenstein. 1982. Screenprint. 38 3/8 x 27 1/8 in. © Estate of Roy Lichtenstein.

He also made prints, ceramics, and huge murals. His *Mural with Blue Brushstroke* is over six stories high!

Goldfish Bowl II, by Roy Lichtenstein. 1978. painted and patinated bronze. 39 x 25-1/4 x 11-1/4 in. © Estate of Roy Lichtenstein.

Mural with Blue Brushstroke, by Roy Lichtenstein. 1984-86. Oil and magna on canvas.
816 x 384 in. © Estate of Roy Lichtenstein.

By the time Roy Lichtenstein died in 1997, he had become one of the world's best-loved artists. His carefully painted images of comic-book scenes and everyday objects are fun to look at, amusing, and beautiful all at the same time. Roy Lichtenstein showed people how to relax and look at serious art in a whole new way.

Works of art in this book can be seen at the following places:

Art Gallery of Ontario, Toronto
Art Institute of Chicago
Guggenheim Museum, New York
Metropolitan Museum of Art, New York
Museum of Contemporary Art, Tokyo
Museum of Modern Art, New York
National Gallery of Art, Washington, D.C.
Tate Gallery, London
Yale University Art Museum